Diosa

Written by: Celeste Alyssa Gomez
Original Poetry by: Celeste Alyssa Gomez
Primary Editor: Celeste Alyssa Gomez
Primary Evaluator: Dreima Flores
Special thanks: Joanna Burgos, Virtual Assistant - La Poeta Publications
Company Website: www.lapoetapublications.com
Social Media: @celestealyssagomez (Instagram)

ISBN: 9798998509186
Published by: Alegria Publishing
Book cover and layout by: @mckadamia

CELESTE ALYSSA GOMEZ

Praise for DIOSA

"Each poem is a carefully placed brushstroke on a canvas of the human experience, blurring the lines between sorrow and solace, memory and hope. Gomez invites us not to merely read, but to feel the subtle tremor of truth in every line. Her poems offer a delicate yet firm exploration of vulnerability, demonstrating how profound strength can emerge from introspection and the patient examination of emotions, perceptions, and personal experiences. Discover your own reflections within her powerful, intimate verse."

— Jean-Pierre Rueda, Author of Amor Entre Aguaceros/Love Between Downpours

"Reading DIOSA made me feel deeply connected to myself. It's hard to explain, but it gave me a renewed sense of identity and reflection. It felt like looking into a mirror while reading the words, especially as a Latina. The sections, RECOLLECTION and RIPE resonated with me the most. Each stirred emotions—anger, happiness, and gratitude—for different reasons.

Witnessing the creation of DIOSA behind the scenes and seeing how much heart Celeste poured into every page was truly incredible. It's been an honor. I'm beyond excited for others to experience DIOSA and feel the same powerful emotions I did while reading each poem. I know they'll find pieces of themselves within its pages."

— Joanna Burgos, Virtual Assistant, La Poeta Publications

"Celeste Alyssa Gomez's Diosa is a gorgeous exploration of femininity, bodily autonomy, and reclamation of power. With conciseness and brevity, she moves with ease between poems about the physical manifestations of love, to poems about mental illness, grief, and healing. Her work most shines when she is defiant and unyielding against past abusers, nay-sayers, lovers. Yet she is also unafraid to be vulnerable as she misses her mother, mourns for her hometown, and asks for help. Throughout the collection, she gives the reader permission to be both soft and strong, delicate and a force to be reckoned with. That, her poems argue, is what makes us all truly diosas."

— Sofía Aguilar, Author of amor

"I loved being part of the process of DIOSA because I enjoyed being part of a diverse/women-led team. DIOSA is not only about the author's experiences/emotions, but it's about representation for the Latino/a community, in particular for women of color. My favorite section definitely had to be 'Cycles', because it explores different emotions for women of color in both personal relationships and in the outside world. We dived deeply into physical insecurities, bullying, and self-empowerment. Topics that aren't usually spoken of because of the fear women will face as they become vulnerable through writing.

It's important to have writers like Celeste share their experiences because without them, we don't have leaders in the community for young women to look up to. Without them we don't inspire future generations. We don't give a voice to those who are afraid to speak up. I love how raw and authentic DIOSA is."

— Dreima Flores, Primary Evaluator, La Poeta Publications

"Young poets like Celeste Gomez remind us that poetry is a sacred alchemist always inviting us to reflect, heal & spread our wings."

— Davina Ferreira, Alegría Publishing Founder & Writer

"Celeste's work is raw and vulnerable in a way only she can express. She dives into her stories unafraid, honoring herself and the women she represents with confidence. Her stories platform the lives of women like her; LA-raised, proud Latinas, Diosas everywhere. They are real, important, and an essential addition to the L.A. poetic canon."

— Efren Castro, Writer

"Diosa is a collection of poetry rooted in empowerment, where every page invites the reader to celebrate the author's strength. From *honoring origin and family to reclaiming identity and growth, Celeste creates space for the reader to love, grieve, and transform their own experiences into resilience. Diosa is both a tribute to heritage and a call to rise into your own power."*

— Raquel Reyes-Lopez, Author of Born To Electrify

"Celeste's words illuminate the power of being a woman—grieving the girl within while reclaiming the strength to become anew. Once we embrace that power, love flows with greater ease. Diosa reminds us that the goddess within is always ours to awaken."

— Solany Lara, Author of Hija de mi padre

DEDICATION

To my life partner, love, and above all, shining light
Your support filled every page I wrote
Thank you for showing me what love feels like again

TABLE OF CONTENTS

CYCLES 15

HEART 83

RIPE 123

RECOLLECTION 175

HOME 221

CYCLES

— i'm the cycle itself and also the diosa that can break from it

the goddess that is my pussy
is the strongest force to provide life,
pleasure, it can be a better partner,
the being your tongue travels to,
to suckle on its sweetness
it doesn't crave your affection
it's powerful as it sits all
in its glory

diosa

when i cry as an adult
the mijita in me is the one crying

mija

what if
is the second most replayed phrase
that is always on my mind
it has been the metaphysical being
to cast premonitions before something
good or bad
what if
is the phrase that heightens my anxiety
what if
you hurt me, they hurt me, or i get nowhere
and it's not meant to be
all the time, effort, and passion i put out
something i don't deserve
what if
i don't deserve it all
because i don't feel good enough
but
i want to see more people who look like me
out here

what if

i'm a person of color
unfortunately i have to encounter setbacks
that some will never understand
even if they were to wear my shoes for day
they'd never break them in

color

i don't get to *opt-in* to be mexicana
my skin can't shed like a cicada
those creatures shed molts when they become adults
when i grow up i *just can't opt-out in being mexicana*
it's who i am and what i'm proud to be
the hardworking feet of mis ancestors hiked obstacles to be here
to give me the life i have
thus our ancestry and culture will reign for generations to see
we scream
we bleed
color
the choice of opt-in and opt-out for diverse literature
proves the racist ideologies that seek to fuel this country
but they will be challenged
as we continue to fight for our freedom to read stories that
represent us

opt-out/opt-in

pride is the mother that birthed you
it will easily create you
as it will end you

the fate of pride

my poetry is an intimate conversation you enter with me
something lyrical, magical, and imaginable
where language can be stretched, exhausted, and broken
like how my tongue still feels with english

my poetry

if you're able to reach me
it's gentle, tame, and meek
my smile is the deadliest thing you see
the rhythm
it circulates neutral tones
we began yellow
and ended gray

reach

in this season of stillness
romancing the little gifts life gives me
the gift to dissect and freeze moments
with people i love most
is a blessing i don't want to take for granted anymore

stillness

you've told me to leave the situation
to find my self-worth
yet when i was trying to do so
all *you* ever did was judge me
to *you* i could never be healed
i was broken to you
so you could find a way
to belittle me
you were never my friend to begin with

belittle

when you work so hard to change and grow
yet they want you to become what they need
is a reflection of unresolved healing

unresolved

he did not love me
he never did
and
the excuses that were given
were a prime example of why i stayed so long
to find control at my lowest
was his personal conviction
to gaslight became essential like air
for this game we called *love*

conviction

i wasn't the tea
you'd sip on to bring comfort
i wasn't warm enough
to touch those delicate lips
i wasn't warm enough
to carry the sun with me
all of it withdrawn from me
turning me into gravel
i wasn't warm enough
because i took what i had left with me
when i walked away from you

warmth

how to leave the toxic relationship
is an entanglement that is rooted from
previous memories before the love became deceptive
it's difficult to turn your eyes from someone you planned a
future with
one where your families got along
their siblings were already calling you *hermana*
to leave all of that and all that time accrued
but
it was the best decision for myself
my future with this man was viewed like this
we'd have a large farm with lots of animals
scenic and quiet - away from the world
to be isolated with just him and whatever family we'd procreate
it was all of this that i became comfortable with

i lost so many friends
because they didn't want to keep up with this bullshit of a life
i thought i was okay with
each day would get lonelier and he'd treat me like shit
ugly
bitch
stupid whore
to leave this relationship became a survival tactic

so i left him and all of this behind
he could not control me anymore
i became okay with being alone for the rest of my life
if it meant that i could be happy and myself
leaving a toxic relationship was the hardest and scariest
moment of my life because i thought i'd be so broken to heal on
my own
running so far
gave me the chance to grow up and become the woman i
intended to be
i promised myself
to never let any man ever mistreat, yell, abuse, or rape me again

never
never
never
and you shouldn't either
so leave them and make a safety plan
create a trusted circle of friends to help you
be kind to yourself
let yourself cry and grieve the relationship if needed
do all of this to get out
your life is much more valuable than the fantasy we create in our
head
so get out
and
leave

leave

to grow up with *her* and speak with her daily is a challenge
like most, *she* doesn't adapt to change well
unfortunately *she* views things as black and white
she can't help it
she's the o.c.d. that chimes in my brain
let me give you a warm welcome to *duro*
somos las duras realidades del otro
duro is spunky and well-organized
however, *duro* can easily get flustered
when control isn't at the pawn of *her* hand
she's been like this from childhood to adulthood
prior to seeking therapy the idea of change such as plans, people,
and even puberty
was a struggle
because *she* wants me to stay put to be safe
yet
i want to live my life
so, the sudden quality to become adaptive to things that
don't go according to plan
has taken time to master
there are moments where *she* struggles
but i hold onto *her*
because *she's* ultimately a part of me
and *she* deserves love too
she's mi duro

duro

together
duro and i aren't broken
i grab *her* hand to remind *her* of
the strengths and struggles we've battled together
it makes us full and human
she completes me as the mujer i continue manifesting into
i'm able to live a full life and do things i thought i never could
i'm able to choose love that's right and healthy for me
i'm able to experience pleasure without fear
i'm able to drive a car and take myself on dates
i can do all of this because i am not broken
if anything i'm healed

together

dare to love and remember to pray

mama whispered to me

you are the life i get to witness from above
don't shut out the ones who matter

as this dream manifests itself in human form
i hear her voice reminiscing about lessons she'd taught me
at this age now
i feel at times i forget what she sounds like
i'm in this periodic cycle where i've built this barrier
that refuses to allow others inside
it became an unhealthy routine
with this barrier it personified itself as a protector and weapon
when those tried to knock it down
it flourished into *mean* brick
making it untracable to find me

barrier

sorry should transform itself into a verb
because it needs to be the action
that gives someone true remorse
not just repetitive words
for us to hear

sorry

o.c.d. is a mental illness
it's not a trend
it's not quirky
it's not just being tidying
it's something that anxiously affects the brain on a daily basis
i'm not ashamed to verbalize how living with o.c.d. is
if only it could be seen and treated
as a real illness like physical ones

living with o.c.d.

the moment i'm alone
i take off the mask i'm wearing
to be just exhausted
to be just somber
when will this character i play stop
so i can be happy

masking

it is not my job to prove
myself to you
a soul like mine
can be imitated, studied,
and mimicked
but there's only one me
and i know my worth

soul

i was so convinced that i could fix everything
even on the edge of the cliff where you would
let me fall
violence was love i grew up and used to witnessing
whether it was romantic or platonic
i was so convinced that i could fix everything

convinced

to release all the anger and anxiety
i felt
i first had to acknowledge them
and take care of myself
the first thing i did was therapy

therapy

Diosa

sadly even when you left
i entered into a cycle of
continuous pain
i settled for what i knew
it took years to get over you
the amount of control you built in my brain
took strength and comfort from loved ones
to unlearn
to finally be me

me

can we even consider it love
when they were a master of
love bombing to begin with

love bombing

mourning the past
killed my mind
making it into art
where i can connect
with others
it healed my heart and soul

past

the friendships
i thought i could trust
slowly turned to increasing
levels of abuse
where manipulation became
the root
and i was too blind to believe it

friendships can be abusive too

there are many days i'll sit in my car
i mute the music and hear the sounds around me
i sit and take this moment to cry
i feel alone
since no one knows what or how i truly feel
i wish i could say something
but my brain automatically tells me that no one
wants to hear negative thoughts

how o.c.d. impacts my daily life

i feel that i've failed everything and everyone
it's an unseen pain that silently drowns me
it's stronger and thicker than rain

rain

how naive i was to think life would be easy
i was fooled by someone who said they'd take care of everything
i took the bait and fell into their game

temptation

dating after a breakup
don't
jump into something rapidly
i tell myself
the therapy appointments
consumed by the crumbled tissues
can be comforting
but
i still feel empty
sometimes i need human intimacy
to have someone love me with no ulterior motive

dating things

mourning is the price given
when the heart allows itself to love

to love

why am i heartbroken
over a love that ceased to exist
delusion
is what you were
and
it knew when to strike
when i was most vulnerable

delusional

do not beg me to stay
because you know deep down i will
with the articulation of your tongue
it twirls and signals an enticing sound
do not beg me to stay
because you know i will break myself in half for you
no matter the amount of times you've chipped at my heart
i will constantly break it for you
so don't bother me anymore
let me be

let me be

i'm allowed to express my feelings
in any way that is healthy and healing for me
whether it's poetry or through a trusted confidant
i'm allowed to speak
indeed
it didn't matter when you expressed all your abuse onto me
if you didn't want me talking about it
then perhaps you should've been better
if you want people not to think negatively of you
then perhaps you should've been better
my words are only on paper
while your words marked a scar in me

speak freely

there is no love like mine
you've found small parts of me
in *her*
i made you feel the way music does
constantly on repeat
no matter how old the track is
new art still finds a way to connect with the primary

my music

i loved you enough
to compromise and sacrifice for you
and
all i asked was your trust in return
tell me
why was that so hard

tell me...

it was possible for him
to love and hate me at the same time
it wasn't new to me
something i fell familiar to
because these were constant feelings
i felt for myself daily
to view my body
criticizing each component
instead of honoring
the art that is me
if it wasn't my words
it was his

pov

how love tastes
it's a hunger that completes you
you decided to lust over *her*
when you had me
tell me
how come when you tasted *her*
your mouth still craved more
you chose to want to love me
way too late
and
now you're left starving

starved

the broken version of myself
has also become one of the most powerful
she has taught me that i can handle
the most difficult obstacles
and
still walk out like a queen

queen

i'm done receiving your flowers
the same ones that you gave to others
i'm not someone's second option
let this be a lesson
that i don't need someone
to pour into me
to make my vase full
i've been capable to do this for myself
all along
remember that

vase

to grieve him
meant that i still loved him
and
those feelings left long ago
the grief he has for me isn't mutual

grief

they ask if my poetry is real
yet
it was very real when *their* words
were used to execute me
to make me feel ashamed,
angry, to feel something
so what's the difference

poetry

it's not cute or romantic
if they want to keep you all to themselves everytime
to seclude you from your friends and family
it is the beginning of a nasty mold
that forms into acts of manipulation,
abuse, and control
it is a mold
that is hidden and will root you down
if you let it
it is also a mold that you have the power
to dispose of by not entertaining it anymore

mold

he must like recylcing content
because i saw him use those same *tricks* to please me
he must like being mediocre

mediocre

your eyes were clearly shut
when sitting near the canvas
the masterpiece you missed out on
was given right in front of you
the paintbrush sat on your hand
yet you refused to put in any effort

canvas

how does the regret
feel when you'd think
i'd be rooted to the cement
of your footsteps
begging for you to open the door
when i'm much stronger than
your eyes perceive
the regret must hurt

the regret

funny
look at this
the phone rings
he calls *me* to tell *me* that he got cheated on
he wanted *me* to make space in my heart for him
and wanted my sympathy
even though that was the same thing he did to me
what a relaxing thought
to give my love again to him
what a fictitious thought

funny boy

suppose if i were to slip away
pretty and original
he craves a replica
what's sweeter than me
miss azúcar morena
from the touch of his skin
on mine
i'd honestly do myself a service
of exfoliating
the existing dead skin cells
from what our skin made
to finally start over
the sweetness he sucks from me
dehydrates whenever things get heated
crystals breakdown
and
to think
even salt can camouflage itself as sugar

skinned

if i knew what safety felt like
i would've spent less time putting my heart
into men who wanted nothing more
to feel safe starts at home

to feel safe

i took a season off
and so many thought
i'd quit poetry
when in fact it's ingrained
in my dna
they thought i'd shrink
so they yapped
that my words would go nowhere
i'm done with the cheap talk
i just want to know why are my
experiences the talk of your table
i flick my fingers into the atmosphere
and my tone is hypnotic
i'm sorry that the poet broke your heart
but what can i say
i'm really
that girl
i'm living my dreams
i'm representing all my fellow poetas y escritoras
because i'm that girl

that girl

Diosa

he tasted it all
each raw and crease soft edge of my body
now he's on your plate
hungry?
just remember when you're
eating him
you're tasting me too
and
the storyline written
and you can gladly have him
i've lost my appetite when it comes to cheaters

taste

dear 25,
you've been one hell of year
walking through a lavender haze
delicate and melancholy
cemented within the fog

dear 25,
this became the year of renewal
entering mid twenties
and feeling blessed and fine like wine
healing burns that overwhelmed me
not letting anxiety creep up on me as it once did

dear 25,
finding out what the hell do i delve onto next
feels like a checklist
finding a career that makes me happy
that makes sense for me
sometimes working somewhere just to cover bills

dear 25,
you also made me feel on edge
the amount of weddings,
babyshowers,
and relationships
convincing me that i had only
a few good years left
that this was some end goal
to reach before soaring into thirties

dear 25,
why does this *topic* feel more sensitive to women
it is exhausting that men are given the opportunity
to have a different outlook when it comes to marriage and
children
its perceived that men yield the power with age
and we have to constantly worry and feel pressured

dear 25,
you are about to see what i accomplish
with the many years i have to face
you have been the groundwork period
as i get into formation
to tackle now and what's beyond thirties

dear 25,
get ready to see me unfold
and reveal the freeing, natural, nasty, outspoken,
beauty of a woman that is me
i'm that antique cabinet
that you stash your brown sugar
soy azúcar morena
my sweetness is endless

dear 25,
my parents married near or close this age
and started their family
but it was their dream
now it's time to live mine

dear 25

what i have is better than money
but you see
there's something he doesn't know
and it's that the love i give is far richer than money
it's not something you're able to replenish easily
love from me has been expended, drained, spirited,
vivid, captivated, and simply spellbound
my love is richer than money
it's more vital than the money he will obtain

more than money

i'm the problem with this issue that feels like a never-ending
dilemma
i stare at the plate of food presented
it seduces me, but i resist to finish my plate
everyone else i know is so beautiful
then there's me
i feel like a huge monster
i thought i had a healthy relationship with food, but truly, i
don't
i'm the problem
by not giving my body the fuel it needs

self-hatred

i just want to be in a mental space where i can enjoy food again
starvation felt like the key component
to achieving the body i wanted
and
now from all the years of doing so
i'm not sure when i'm even full anymore

full

relationships are like mirrors
they're capable of showing what
you think and believe about yourself

what we see and what we don't

you might have been the first one
i loved
but when i truly
found the person that deserved to be in my life
the *love* you ever gave to me became fruitless - it was just *parched*

parched

love is peculiar like fruit
you peel certain parts that are good to consume
while others are clear to avoid yet we still consume...

fruit of love

starting over
stretching dollars
became the same motion
as pulling my hair
i was losing hair like money
all from stress

stress

on the days when i refused to move
to even speak or take care of myself
it was the women in my life
that gave me their love
to be there for me
throughout my time of
grief
depression
anger
through it all
the unit we built was *hermanahood*
they got me back to my feet
to provide life in me
as if it were water
their support was essential
they became mis hermanas

hermanahood

the love from my friends
is the same as familial
it's community
it's magic we create
and
it's something i never knew i needed
when life drains me

community

the next time he tells you
that he's *unsure* about you
remind that boy
of how lucky
he had it
when he was able to sit
front row as a special guest
to experience
the broadway show that is *you*

broadway

your soft moments
are just as powerful
as your forte

softness is powerful

HEART

— you became the first love that doesn't make me question

let's start from the beginning
she's nineteen wearing a university tee
patiently waiting in the community dorm hall
not knowing she'd be meeting the love of her life
she turned her face towards him
there's this cute boy in a baseball cap and joggers
i wonder what his voice will sound like
what will he think of me
she thought
he smiles and approaches the couch to sit next to her

so you're the person that needed help with your video project right
i nod excitedly even if it could be a lie
it's so nice to meet you, talk me through this video idea you have

what was supposed to be a twenty-minute convo
turned into hours of talking to 4:00 AM
a series about relationships, classes, majors, dorm life,
where we're from and dreams

little did we know this was just the beginning because...

he left quite an impression

the beginning

before our paths crossed
i had already dreamt about you
i was already writing about you before you came into my life
this was a love that transcended right before we spoke
a love as powerful as this comes only once in a lifetime
especially when we least expect it

pathway to each other

we remained friends for four years
speaking here and there
we'd bump into one another often
i'd see you running across canyon crest
the crosswalk that stood between us felt like a ocean
we'd wave to each other quietly
sometimes you'd run my way
the few times you stopped in front of me
i nearly forgot to communicate
the wet glands dripped so satisfyingly from your face
it fell gently on the floor
you'd ask
how are you doing
i'd respond with *fine*
when in reality i wasn't
i was unhappy
i knew i'd never have a chance with someone like you
i was just your friend
and
that was that

just friends

i didn't want to be your friend anymore
so i did my best to get over you
i kept my conversations short
even though i tried
you found your way to unravel me
break me open to devour all my attention
you pulled me as your rope
and
untied my knots ever so gently
listening to each tangle, twist, whirl, and splice that i held inside
this only strengthened our bond

bond

i will admit
when you spoke to me about the
current person you were dating at the time
i was a bit jealous
but
i was also glad to see you with someone that made you happy
you were my friend when i needed you
so i wanted to do the same in return
you deserved it

friends

time fast forwards and i'm single
yet you're with someone else so i give up
on what it could've been
for the first time i tell myself i don't need another man's intimacy
to make me whole
this is where i learn to heal and love myself

whole

for some reason you started looking at me differently
at least in my head it felt like it
i remember the summer going into our senior year of college
we were texting non-stop
during a trip to nueva york you kept sending me pictures and
updates
it felt so nice to feel included in *your life*
i kept thinking that maybe we should give this a try
little did i know where we'd be...

nueva york

i kept thinking that if i tell you my feelings
would this be something *i even want*
this was my first time being single for this long
giving myself space to focus on me
i thought about myself and what i want for my life
it wasn't tied to someone else for once
did i want to ruin a good friendship
was my biggest question...

the uncertainty (risk)

by the universe we're both single at the same time
my heart tells me to give *it* one last chance
so
i tell you how i feel and it's reciprocated
we seal this new love with a kiss
i love how your hand grips my neck
the way your fingers stir through my hair
how much bigger your body is to mine
it tunnels its way inside me
fingers crossed so tightly
and
this is how we end our first night of many

the first night

i look forward to the time
we move in together
where we can lay in bed
each and every night
to share meals in front of one another
instead on facetime or on the weekends
to brush our teeth in the same mirror
spit the toothpaste and turn our head
to glance at one another as we smile
to have a hug with you in real time
when there's a bad situation
to have this all on repeat
i can't wait for all of this
to be just us
to love loudly or quietly
at our disposal
because it will be our space together

repeat

naturally i'm going to write about you
about our love, poems and poems
that make me smile and blush
words that are as thick as my tongue
to design its own library
this is a love i've never experienced before
and
it's my favorite story to re-read and study

study

interesting how the world is
we came from two completely different areas
yet
we're also connected by the city *pico rivera*
not many know of this city when i mention it
and
to hear you causally namedrop the road names
was satisfyingly pleasing to my ear
i could hear you speak all day
who knows maybe we saw each other prior to college
i think the universe was waiting for the right moment to
introduce us to one another

connection

hello... ?
hello... ?
a word we came familiar with
when speaking on the phone
you could hear the city life behind me,
roommates, dishes placed in the sink,
glasses clanking, machines beeping
everything you could hear because i wanted you to
i wanted you to hear all parts of me
and
you gladly listened

phone calls

the sound of your voice doesn't even
have to crawl underneath the door
the noise from your footsteps
has me floating as my clothes disappear
and
candles lit on the floor are ready
to suddenly be blown away from what we will do next

i want it

Diosa

i want to be the love you
dream and hunger for each morning
where you're laying in between the sheets
longing for my companionship
where you're able to lay your face
on my sweet bum
and i allow your hands to take over
i want to be the love you
send and save the voice memos of
the love that i receive texts of the
simplest yet worldly updates
where i can already tell you're smiling
when typing
i want to be love that doesn't have you
feel like you're settling
but is thriving right next to you
the type of good, experimental,
boundary-setting, funny,
nasty, rare to this world,
still eye-shocking, and
true form of love
i want to be all of that
the love that
streams already within
your dna
it is as coiled
through the same
length from our fingers that kiss one another
the love that
we don't always have to touch
and if i were to disappear
you'd be able to find me
from our signs
you'd be able to find me
i want a love as powerful
and rich as that

a love just as rich

when his fingers first dipped inside me
he noticed the blood
how my honey can be sweet golden
to rich red
the power i have to bleed so much
and
not die
is one of the many glories of *diosa*

sweet red

her face softened from
the grip of his touch
making her eyes roll
slowly back
he eventually rested near
the royal gates of *diosa*
waiting to enter
by her command
he made his entrance

oral pleasure

i want your lips
to travel to other
luxurious places on my body
i want your lips to taste
the chilling and exciting
gift that is my body
it's tingling as if an icicle were
sliding on our backs

the excitement

when *diosa* is soaked
she waits for him to dive into her ocean
he tells me he's big
bigger than who *me*
no way
i might stroke the ego just a bit longer
it's just a rule of the game isn't it
the power of my sea can create mankind
nothing is bigger and bolder than *diosa*
it's a force to be reckoned with

our power

we release at the same time
as my hips activate
they curve into a beautiful sculpture
you view in the getty
eyes close gently
we pass out softly

orgasm

she became the music
he loved to listen to daily
with intent and care

music

look me in the eyes
as your lips plant *besos*
in the realm of *diosa*
the presence
is
breathtaking

besitos

he is in need of water
he rows his tongue inside
toward sustenance
drinking the sweet wetness for his life

nourishment

crazy to think
that we live together
spend each micro moment
doing what couples be doing
yet
the moment your body exits
the front door
i instantly miss you

to live with someone

there will never be enough
hours of the day to say
i love you
i hope this phrase travels
through various realms
to reach you
even when we disappear
i hope my words
find you in any lifetime
we fall in

lifetime

the sound of your laughter
is much more pleasing than
the orgasm itself
it is long-lasting
and more authentic

his sound

he enriches this part of my life
to be growing with me
is what i crave

growth together

our dates together
still feels like a honeymoon
five years later
and
the conversations are still as if we first met

five and many more

let me take us back to the year of lockdown
i sat on my air mattress of my apartment
anxiously waiting for our video call
it was our eighth virtual date
we planned to stream the *notebook* together
i stayed up the night before finding the perfect outfit to wear
even though we weren't seeing each other in person
you'd probably only see my neck up
i wanted
no
i needed to look perfect
funny that a virtual date can feel just as stressful as an in-person
one
our virtual dates consisted of movies, tea, dinner, anything to get
through the first glimpse of the pandemic

lockdown

on my birthday i got covid
i was scared because i knew of people who passed away from
covid
you reassured me throughout the whole process
i remember on christmas you brought me food since i could taste
again
our hands with gloves
our fingers poking through the gate that separated us
masks covering our smiles
we used our eyes to communicate
this was the first act of kindness anyone ever showed me
it was new to me like one learning to ride a bicycle
yet
its one of the memories i look back on most - at times when i feel
that i'm not enough

acts of kindness

our privacy is scared
it's the house we build
we can create a strong foundation
or let it crumble easily

privacy

the communication we built
matured into the oxygen
we breathe

air

love isn't always the honeymoon phase
it's choosing to love the other person
through all stages of life
during my seasons of built up depression and anger
he still chose to love me unconditionally
i'd lock myself in the room to cry
i didn't want to be near anyone or him
i'd wish he'd wipe his entire memory of me
i felt as if i didn't deserve him
yet
he stayed close and listened to me
when we laid in bed he held onto me closer
kissed my neck and said *goodnight i love you*
it was these small gestures
that helped me get to the next day
to see each other's rawest emotions
and
to still support one another
this is what i call love
a love that is not only rich but rare
something i never want to let go of
i pray that our hearts, physical touch, and minds
are cemented to one another
in all lifetimes
because he chooses to love me daily
i choose to do the same and love him whole heartedly

love is

the partner i'm with
is one that is building a home with me
not for me
they're secure and honest
their love language is making
sure i feel safe

partnership

i created a library
of all the pages we created
i turned them into books
that sat on the shelves
a history of our journey
they didn't collect dust
they were taken care of
with the same kindness and love
you give me

library

there's love in silence
sometimes even louder than our actions
to feel complete even through silence
is some sort of magic we learn
not speaking a word as we occupy the same space
we automatically grab the other's hand for a kiss
we pick up after the other
bring a second plate without hesitation
it's the peace we bring one another
and
i hope we grow into decades later doing the same thing

silent love

thank you for opening your heart to me
when i included us in my soul
it restored a ruptured wound i buried deep down

thank you

RIPE

— i rebel by avoiding poisonous fruit that stores the seeds of those disguised, i only seek ones where i grow ripe and rich

i became the soaring dove
noticing the changes around me
with the calling wind
remembering to follow my purpose

dove

my first failure
won't be my last
it'll be from these mistakes that i learn and grow from
it is what remodels me into becoming ripe

remodel

Diosa

just because i know how to keep it together
doesn't mean i'm not hurting either
sometimes i like to cover up my stress
by adding extra work because that's all i can think about
it's something i want to change with myself so i can open up to
say i need help

help

i've already had everything at the tips of my fingers
and will gain more of it
because as women we are told that there's a limit
when the whole world has been ours to begin with

ours

the words spoken from my mouth
are a powerful tool when addressing myself
it's as if a shadow has come and cut my tongue
because of all the negative self-talk i give
i need to start talking to myself better
but *how* - when my mind
isn't any better

self-talks

a poet's tongue i hope you trust
to live, breathe, and write in los angeles
is a beautiful thing
a poem for my hometown
to be a proud Angeleno
in the city
that can be anything you want it to be
is now experiencing a burned vessel
the fires have heavily
impacted and completely destroyed
many homes, schools, organizations, and memories
while we mourn together
we rely on our community to hold us tight
we join forces to create resources and funds
to rebuild those lives affected by the ashes
we thank the first responders and firefighters
by being on the front line to help save
what we have of our city
we've lost angels
angels have been injured
as we gather together to heal our wings
we pray for LA
we love you LA

LA

if driving is the most LA of experiences
then i live for mi carro
mi carro has cruised down in all hours of the night
to find a gorgeous view paired with comfort food
to be in the city where it's anything you imagine it to be
the lights are in front of you gleaming and screaming
as if they're calling your name
you breathe in the air
this experience is shared by oneself or with close friends
we wear our city by the same expression as wearing your heart on
your sleeve
something magical when you're surrounded by community

city life

i want to experience us running on
the meadow green grass that has a hill
we hold each other's hand to keep momentum
once we make the top
we lay down viewing the skyline
you grab the flowers near you to place in my hair
summers like this are what i long for
but
each season has to change and move on

summer

somos la voz y el cambio
para nuestra comunidad,
cuando luchamos juntos, ganamos
aqui estamos y no nos vamos

I.C.E. out of our home

we're all born beautiful
all living and breathing
so
at what age do people get to decide
that we're considered *ugly*
when we just started experiencing what life is

we're all born beautiful
to enter life with the mindset
that sees ourselves as *ugly*
is the biggest contradiction

life is beautiful so why aren't we...

beautiful

beyond my skin
beyond my voice
beyond my education
there's a human

beyond

i am allowed to stare at the mirror
and
love myself even if you don't like me
i am allowed to accept the changes of my body even if you don't
apparently it's so *fucking irritaring* to people
for me to not give an explanation as to why i've changed
whether it be smaller or larger
they like to keep tabs on me because they're the chismosos they
are
the problem isn't me
it's the fact that you have unhealed wounds you're trying to cast
on me
listen closely
i don't care
i write words that burn
my flame is only getting brighter and brighter for those to see

burn

does my wit animate you
does my voice stimulate
something in you
does it come as a surprise
to see these eyes
that have grown so wise
to stand here
from those who continue to mock me
because they tell me that i'm not deserving of poetry
that a brown girl
that is me
should be doing something better with her time
and
tell me what would *you* prefer for me to do
would it be serving a *man*
because by your stereotype that's what *you* think
i should be doing
the very fact that a woman of color is doing something different
bothers *you*
well it will come to your surprise
that the way i serve is with my voice
my conviction
my emotion
and i rise
i rise against *you*
to galvanize this feeling

i rise

poetry is daily
poetry is universal
it is color, expression, prayer,
it is anything we want it to be
the beauty that poetry gives us
to transform itself for our vision
it makes me feel sexy and confident
it completes me as a woman
it is the obsession i crave

poetry is...

write
write it all
i told myself
you deserve to heal
it's time to put yourself first

write, write, write...

when i hold back
i'm not allowing myself to live up to my potential
i want you to deplete the whole area in front of you
like no one's watching

your grounds

the most complicated
relationship we will ever have
is with ourselves
take time to really understand
what you want in life
and who you want in your life

me (you)

the snap of my fingers operate
an enticing sound
the same magical feeling
as my fingers dance for me
to give *diosa* a performance
worth climaxing

by oneself

they viewed her as *weird* and *ugly*
they did everything in their power
to throw boulders, rocks, and stones at her
as she continued to climb the mountain
each finger gave its all as it held its grip
this act of fortitude
angered them more
so they gathered a group to throw more
yet
she kept climbing
you should see her fingers
you would think they were from years of playing guitar
when they're from life itself
all the *fucking shit* she faced
and
the *diosa* that she is
she keeps soaring

soar

interesting how the inner workings of *diosa*
still seems like a taboo subject
if the word *pussy* makes you feel uncomfortable
then good
i want it to
because you claiming my *pussy*
while i walk on the street
makes me uncomfortable
makes us uncomfortable
to hear you objectify us
and
target us like we're something to be owned
makes all of us feel unsafe
so your ears better listen when i say *pussy*
because it's mine not yours

pussy

these last two years have been the most beautiful, confusing, and frustrating moments of my life from unlearning negative energy that consumed my entire body to setting boundaries with those who like to suck on every fiber of my being; i've learned that certain people and feelings are only temporary such as breakups with friends, ones who want to constantly compete and deter you down instead of walk beside you, these type of memories are dried flowers that i no longer wish to water; i fold them into a book that finally ended, i think of now and where my next few years of my twenties will take me and will i be happy with the outcome; i revisit my goals often and reflect on where i've come so far, it's a weird feeling to be in mid-twenties because you're in a place where it's not young or old, you're just floating - so many tell me that thrifty is flirty and thriving, but all i can do is wait till i get there and focus on the age i am now - i feel like people are scared to share about failing, yet that's something i feel has helped me learn more about myself, when certain things i expect didn't come into fruition, it drew me back to the board to revise the plan; old enough that my frontal lobe has grown and i'm a woman, yet i still feel like a teenager living an adult life, old enough to see and witness the scary and painful results of the election and what 2025 has come to with the vile person we have as a president - to see how the world wants to tear families of color apart and get rid of mental health resources is terrifying - to be in the middle of 2025 now and wonder what will the next season bring

change

i'm a sister and friend to many
i'm a partner
but
the question is will i ever be mother
am i capable
to have my own
it is fear i have
that i will die before my child
mine did
it has taken years to heal
so
i don't know if i'll ever be mother
time will tell

time will tell

Diosa

in another universe
we're reading poetry to one another
all day and everyday
not giving a damn on what's outside
we are eachother's safe space
we sit on the green grass of a mountain
pouring words to one another
feeling refreshed and renewed
this is what a poet's community feels like

a poet's community

to see the color of the leaves turn
another season has passed
this is what wild solitude smells like
to mediate and not be disturbed
are rare moments nowadays
to be with oneself
is always a retreat

retreat

Diosa

the library we build
is an archive of all our
longings
where it's endless wonder
to feed off our ideas and dreams
this is the start of building
a generation of our own

archives

i love and appreciate women differently
than a man would
than my father would
i don't manipulate them
i don't invalidate their feelings
i still hunger to be around them
but
it is a hunger for wanting to know their
wisdom, courage, and strength
it is a type of hunger
that gives respect to them
to be around a circle of women is powerful
if only most men would understand this
if only most men would respect us women

us women

trusting the uncertainty is worrisome
but
i pray and hold the universe close to my heart

prayer

the most crucial moments i need
are to lean into *her*
the new version of myself
that grew from all of the mistakes
i'll find myself
tapping into the old version
the *mijita* that approached life so meekly
i'll find myself
forgetting the *mujer* i am
and dressing into that insecure *mijita*
i once was

the layers of clothes that bury me

i was so interested in showing you how happy i was
that i lost the reason for what made me truly happy

lost

in my head
it constantly spirals the three phrases
i am deep breathing
i am safe
i am present
the three have become mechanized
even when it's not true
that's how it feels to ride
front seat on autopilot

autopilot

you make me feel so wanted and loved
that the stress of death haunts me
i want you close
near
as i organize these thoughts to safety

close

death is a reminder that each day
we have together is a gift
let us be intentional with our time
let every kiss last five seconds more
let every moment we spend
be cherished
as we grow in our love
i want my face to have so many
creases from all the smiles and laughs
we share
i want you to remember me for how much
i loved you as you loved me

expiration

rediscover yourself in silence
sit with your emotions and listen
as if you were on a stage
spotlight ready to shine
drown the noise
and go on your performance

solo act

the stronger version of yourself
has gambled heartbreak, grief, and
sudden changes
it's mature, complete, and golden
it has cultivated its own muse
it is ripe

ripe

light the candles and dance in the center
your soul is empathic and healing all at once
you revisit the nostalgia while in the moment
smiling from those who've stayed in your path
and even laugh at some things your heart dedicated time to
you're not hard on yourself like you once were
you are embracing all that is you

a day alone

in between where i want to be
and where i am currently
is a constant mind game that
stimulates my anxiety
the waiting is so slow
i am able to count the seconds from my breath
the stillness is relearning patience

in-between

a reason to keep going is because
i am supposed to do something greater
than what others say
maybe it's okay that i feel lost
and that i don't have all the answers
i'm only human
a reason to keep going is because
i have to trust in myself
even when others don't
it's my job to trust in me
not theirs

a reason

different ways i've abandoned myself
without even realizing it was
saying *yes* to certain situations or people
when i wanted to say *no*
or apologizing to someone for something i didn't even do
so i could please and have them talk to me
romanticizing the bare minimum
staying in relationships that have entirely run their course
staying in friendships that tolerated me and were fake
staying quiet from those who have disrespected me
i abandoned the inner mijita that relied on me
the mujer in me has outgrown these bad habits and
is never letting go again

from the mijita to the mujer

my brows
are arcs of wisdom and life
they can communicate anything you need
without a single word spoken

arc

the feet from those who hurt me
are ones that i refuse
to lay underneath
ever again

underneath

trillions of atoms
take their course
throughout my body
with every intent
to keep me alive
i must take care of myself
to put effort and love
as they do daily

trillion

Celeste A Gomez

the way i am able to rise
and
become more ripe from each obstacle
is a wonderful feeling
the point is that i will always be given the opportunity
to rise and that's a beautiful thing to witness

witness the beauty

the interesting thing about love
is how it touches my lips
and
enters my mouth
the taste can be great
but
it's not the same

think about it

the longest thing it took me
to realize is that i was the only
person who can save my own life
it wasn't someone else
i've held the power from within
all these years
it's the people in my life that remind of this power
it's how i was able to save my own life

save myself

i learned that
the candles i light
can also be for celebrations too
its not always something somber

how fire can change

the pain we feel shall pass
no matter how dreadful it might be
no matter how the pain transforms itself
into something bigger then what it used to be
the pain is a void that can increase if you allow
yourself to attach everything else to it

with patience

it requires strength to give kindness
to those who have been malicious towards you

i do my best to serve kindness to everyone in my life
even if they come off bitter
i try to understand why they feel this way
sometimes compassion is what someone needs
since it may have been what they never received

kindness

i shouldn't have to beg you
to give me a proper relationship
i choose to love and have you in my life
if the feeling isn't mutual
then i have no obligation to be your friend
don't call me when something hasn't worked out
or
if you broke up with someone
you weren't there when i needed you nor did you check in
so i cut our friendship a long time ago
yet your ego was too blind to see it

ego

what a blessing it is to grow
into the woman i choose to be
i reflect on the moments where my life
could be so different
whether it was in my career or living in a different city
yet she is and will always be effortlessly timeless
she has shown resilience through change
she is able to climb mountains boldly
she'd be so proud of the mujer i've grew into
in the mid-twenties era
soon to be thirties
what a blessing it is to grow
into the woman i choose to be
to have my friends beside me
we age with one another
soaring into the next era
chismosas y cafecito
displaying that we are *diosas*
in every stage of life
this is the gift of aging
to become the finest version of myself
is something magical

finest version of myself

RECOLLECTION

— to the mijita that is still learning to love and trust herself unconditionally

she carried me inside her belly
i nested a home
found my ways
to communicate with her
whether it was a kick here or there
i was excited to be held by her
she gave me the opportunity of life
to be taught and loved by her
is still the best gift i ever gotten
and
will never forget
she risked her life to birth me
i don't who is a greater hero
than our mamas

mama's belly

it's been almost a decade
since you've been gone
nine years
the grieving is something that
will never go away
but
it changes shape and flows
differently in my system
whether it was calming
or overwhelming
you were once my rock
and to have you gone
is an obstacle i live with
everyday
i will never stop loving you

mama

in some
the heart will only see the monetary value
that could even happen within family

sad truth

i am from the *man*
who has decided that
now *they* want to be part
of my life
who was absent
but
made their comebacks
well-known whether it would be
jail visits or fights
he acted on the creation
yet the art my parents created
was just an empty canvas to him
we were a whole gallery of art
that he refused to visit

family gallery

he would've been the embodiment
of a father if only he'd given his support
without the law telling him he had to

support

mama asked him
would you want your daughter to date a man like you

i knew at a young age which parent was the problem
the constant cycle of absence and toxicity
was enough for me to realize i deserve respect
yet

mama asked him
would you want your daughter to date a man like you

i was with men that treated me like complete shit
who took advantage of me
one that i took emotional abuse from for four years
the pursuit to put me down
and
paint my life into his vision

i thought i had ran away from men like you
when i was drawing back to square one
because *you* were all that i saw as a man
growing up
you might've been absent, but your actions
transcended into the men i dated
i settled for those who were
masters of the love bomb craft
it took almost taking my life
to stop entering relationships
that represented *you*

now if only mama could ask you one more time
would you want your daughter to date a man like you

father and daughter

the drunken nights on the floor
where he laid naked
from endless bottles of alcohol
i would imagine what a normal
relationship would be like and if we'd have one

alcohol

his excuse was that he was angry
consequently
the multiple times he wrapped his fingers around my neck
snug like glue, hard like clay
it wasn't the first time i thought i was going to die
it was a reoccurring thought based on how he treated us
no
the breaking point was in the car
your temper would rise and so did the speed
from one of those times i thought we would die
i'd picture myself flying out from the car
separated from everyone
the body of a twelve year-old would be found
and
that would've been my life
taken and stolen
all because you could never control your temper
why did we *consider violence as love* for so long

temper

the amount of alcohol didn't matter
the damage he caused didn't matter
getting into a crash from drinking didn't matter
all that did was his escape from it

addiciton

you made it so easy
already teaching me how to live without you

absence

to smile even on the hardest days made me a master of masking

hard days

to forgive is an act of self-liberation, we free ourselves from the trauma and learn to create boundaries

to forgive

grief is a mixture of things
it's like making tamales
the masa that is soft and mushy
are what feel like the first stages
you experience sadness and anger
and
you're vulnerable since you've let down your barrier
hence the softness
but
like tamales, they only become delicious and better
by the strength and help of loved ones
you soak and clean the husks
el corazón es la masa y el cuerpo es la cáscara de maíz
by putting them together you come complete
grief goes through all stages like a tamale
even when it crumbles
you have your loved ones to support and build you back up
grief is love
grief is hard
grief is like a tamale
you will have a whole village by your side to make sure you don't
crumble

crumble

we're not as close as we used to be
we always end up hurting each other
or
fighting constantly in a sentence
we will always be siblings
but
we've matured to walk away from one another

estranged

it was always *why couldn't you be a better sister*
what is your problem with me
always pointing fingers towards me
breaking down the softness of my brain
chewing bits and pieces to piss me off
just never listening
so
i decided i'm just done

done

she was six years old
she was the little girl from pico rivera
she'd get together alongside with other neighborhood children
they'd swimmed in the community pool that felt like a ocean
to be on a donut shaped floatie that cruised through all four
corners of the pool
to wear a life jacket to be safe and secure
then it was time to shower
the water getting warm and the steam covering up the room
he did the unthinkable
she kept her life jacket as a act of safety, but it was no help
it all happened there
for a few times until *he* was caught
he was supposed to protect her
yet
he hurt her and the anger rooted from there
he's just like my father

six

from ages seven to nine
i still don't want him to touch me, hug me, or even look at me
his presence angered me more than anything
we'd go to church, pray, eat and repeat on sundays
i asked god many times *why me*
i was angry at god at such a young age even before double digits
as i got older i suppressed the memory
and
i hated myself
i hated my thighs, stomach, eyes, hair, face, everything
as we sat in church
i'm old enough to altar serve
i looked at golden cross and saw a man hanging
i asked it
when will i start loving myself...

seven

Celeste A Gomez

the nightmares became increasingly worse
the memory and act haunted her endlessly
throughout middle school and high school
she would wish for it to go away
she ran so far until finally confronting it

confrontation

Diosa

i immediately had to begin therapy
so many big words being thrown around
i had no idea what they all meant being so young
but
we needed to talk about what happened and my case for o.c.d.
this became the first evolution of *duro*
she emerged from panic and trauma
that's the best way i could describe why my brain is the way it is
i would panic if anything got on me like nail polish and dirt
i had to be in control of everything
it was something i obsessed over constantly
because it was the first thing no one could take away from me
duro's fixation on counting the food on my plate and washing
my hands fifteen times
was a lot to deal with
but
she wasn't alone because i was with her on finding a solution to
calm down
the control led to tantrums
so many people called me insane when inside i was just a girl
hurting

duro

Diosa

i immediately had to begin therapy
so many big words being thrown around
i had no idea what they all meant being so young
but
we needed to talk about what happened and my case for o.c.d.
this became the first evolution of *duro*
she emerged from panic and trauma
that's the best way i could describe why my brain is the way it is
i would panic if anything got on me like nail polish and dirt
i had to be in control of everything
it was something i obsessed over constantly
because it was the first thing no one could take away from me
duro's fixation on counting the food on my plate and washing
my hands fifteen times
was a lot to deal with
but
she wasn't alone because i was with her on finding a solution to
calm down
the control led to tantrums
so many people called me insane when inside i was just a girl
hurting

duro

195

for what he did
i grew so much anger
he was supposed to protect me
yet
he was another man that *failed* me
when i needed him most
when the men in your family disrespect you
it hurts more

failure

when i give the answers
they toggle the switch in my brain
to hear the words they feel is necessary
switching off my vivid memories like a light bulb

manipulation

the men in my life
would argue that they were *good* to me
let's humor this for a second
if they were *good*
why couldn't they have been great, wonderful, attentive, etc.
why just *good*
why just the bare minimum
that's a crime in itself
when you want a child to remember fond memories of you
then give them reason to

give me a reason to

the social pressure to appear *normal*
really got to me as i grew up in school
i didn't know how to be a *girl* according to people
and
i was afraid to get out of my comfort zone
i did my best to hide under the radar when it came to my o.c.d.
i just wanted people to wish i was like them
i wanted to be able to wear makeup and nail polish and not freak
out
all i truly wanted from them was acceptance

normal

to my mama
that did everything in her power
to provide, love, and guide
i thank you for your patience in me
you taught me that i am capable of
finding people to love me for who i am

lessons

to the mijita in me
you are worthy of being trusted
your experiences from it all
have made you into someone brave

to the mijita in me

growing up in pico
we were called the kids
from saint hills
we'd be together all the time
being chismosos all at once
i was the kid from santa fe
then there were the ones from el rancho
then the others were home schooled
or there were occasional ones that went to st. paul
a wide bunch we all were
they would ask me
you're planning on going to college right
i look over
i don't think i'm smart enough for that
it was a real reality i felt
i said
maybe college isn't meant for me
they would tell me
it's what you make of it

the kids on my block

as a teen i would go to bible study
we'd gather together to talk about
god
i don't think many of us were even paying attention
there was this boy
he swooned me easily
in our conversations and his eye contact
one evening we were near the
bushes by the church
he pulled me close
to kiss me
it was a moment where i didn't
feel scared or disgusted
i felt like a normal teen girl experiencing teen things

skater boy

soy chicana
soy morena
y
it's beautiful
i remember hating
the thickness of my hairy arms
being ashamed of how it made me look
i didn't feel like a mujer
mi mama told me that if i shave it'll grow worse
i couldn't possibly disobey her
so i found so many ways to hide them
i was so focused on growing up so fast
that i didn't take the time to appreciate
being a kid
my hairy arms haunted me all the way up to college
until i got the courage to shave them
and i didn't really feel the difference
i wish i would've just normalized my hair all this time
my hair or no hair never changed the beauty i carry

normalize hair

be who you are
you are beautiful
with every curve, mark,
size, and style you decide
to represent yourself in
your skin is beautiful
because it is and will always be yours to claim
it is your temple from every stage of life

you are

doce
i became of age
mama vouched for me too
and what i meant by that is
i was old enough to handle
a tamale station on my own
we gathered around the island
mama gave me my own cuchara
to spread la masa on the husk
i moved up from bagging to spreading
my love from cooking grew from there
my hands creating cultura y arte

tamales

when i say i love myself
it's when i am dancing
and levitating my hips
to the beautiful sounds
of bachata, cumbia, merengue, hip-hop, etc.
so freely
to embrace it all
i feel me when dancing
it has always been a safe space for me
at the age of eight
i would gather mama's cds
to play on the sony player
dancing to selena to janet jackson
when i'm not writing
estoy bailando

bailando

i'm like mi abuela in many ways
i indulge in sweets that bring a smile to my face
i laugh whole-heartedly that my belly is full
i have an eye when it comes to jewerly
i wear my gold earrings like abuela
i wear a stylish outfit and lipstick knowing i own the room i walk
in
i am confident and beautiful like abuela
i am thankful for mi abuela
she has created generations
without her
we wouldn't be here

i'm like mi abuela in many ways
we have the same humor
we're such chismosas together
i like a good color of nail polish that pops
i cry over sentimental moments
and
as i get older i will one day be as wise as mi abuela
to create a potential bloodline
to grow more into life
now that's something

abuela

cuídate mucho
is the phrase mi abuela y yo say to each other often
whenever i get ready to leave
i used to live at home full-time until i turned eighteen
that's when i headed out for college to be something
i know mi abuela was counting on me
during phone calls and holiday breaks
we'd sit on the couch and be the chismosas that we are
from the raise of her eyebrow
i knew the chisme was going to be good
she'd start telling me the latest of what's happening at church, etc.
and asked if i talked to my own brother lately
in between something sweet like pan dulce or pastel
we'd laugh and cry
during mi abuela's hardest moments
where she fell and injured her ankle from the stairs
she still wanted to find time to be a chismosa
when that happened
she asked me to paint her nails and cut her hair
because even though she wasn't attending church in person anymore
she still needed to look her best
i've never cut someone's else hair before
even though it wasn't the best, abuela still managed to laugh
it's moments like this where i realize how much cuidate is much
more than a saying
it's code for god to keep the other safe so we can keep this
conversation going
as abuela gets older i've seen our couch sessions get shorter or
she asks me to repeat things
she will get tired easily
it's this time i plan to cherish the most
with the biggest and boldest chismosa i know
cuídate mucho
from this lifetime and beyond
to the og chismosa

cuídate chismosa

i prayed to god each night
that we'd buy a home
of our own someday
and
that mama would alive to see it

midnight prayers

i wish i could travel back in time
to see mama when she was in her twenties
i wonder what she was like as a friend
so many tell me
but
to experience it is different
would we get along, would we have the same mannerisms
would she know i was even her daughter
i wonder about the advice she'd give me
i'll never know, but based on what her friends tell me
she was an amazing friend and i hope to be the same to mine

patti

as long as god gives me each day to wake up to
it's a reminder that i'm not done yet

another day

setting boundaries
is an act of self-healing

boundaries

the crying tantrums didn't make me crazy
it was a way to protect myself
from the unfairness

chillona

mijita

i thought i was alone
and
forgotten for such a long time

mijita

mijita

despite what they did to me
all i ever wanted was their love
and support, but i was never good enough
i was always a problem

mijita

mijita

feeling alert all the time
doesn't make you weird
it's from the trauma that
made you hypervigilant

mijita

i've forgiven the past
and have used the sadness
to transform my life to be the one
i deserve to live

onward

i am not what happened to me
i am much more than that
i radiate light and wisdom

radiate

we learn to let go of resentment
for a brighter outlook to find compassion

compassion

HOME

— the home i have is what i searched for a long time

as i grow older
maturing is realizing that my cup is full
when i leave relationships that isolate me
i like to shift my mindset and heart to those
that always include me at the table
make room for me
i like to nurture those who make feel like home

home

these ongoing emotions with my o.c.d.
reside in the home i have
sometimes they never leave the house
when i need to most
these moments are the hardest
because i spend days on the couch
dissociating and letting things pile
i don't eat or speak
i feel anxious to open to others on how i truly feel
my partner witnesses these passings i have
he is patient and reminds me of the strengh i have even when i
forget

passings

when you're bashing another person
based off their looks
you're only fueling the idea of how truly
insecure you feel about yourself
instead of mocking someone else
look into the mirror to connect with the lost pieces you need
to find true healing

insecurities

sex for many people
was an act of love and pleasure
to be naked was to be comfortable with that person
majority of the time
when for me
sex felt like i was in a dangerous place
my innocence being ripped, thrusted, and stretched
sex was something i thought i needed to do to keep love
being the woman i am now
i don't need sex to feel wanted
sex for me now is consent from each party
deliberate orgasms
and
something i can safely say *yes* or *no* to
without being ridiculed

free will

i don't care if you like me
it's not my mission to guide you towards pathways
to be my friend
my friends and loved ones that get me, *get me*
it's healing actually because i'm not wasting time or energy
on things that are so minuscule

i really don't...

please don't throw the term *friend* loosely
your friends are people who are there for you,
they support you and your dreams
they can read how you feel and listen intently
friends are people that want to see you transform
into the best version of yourself
friendships should be selfless not selfish

be careful who you call a friend

duro
calm down
let's stop overthinking
and
over-analzying the situation in our mind
that some things get blurry and we start
making up things that haven't even happened yet
we forecast the future
as if we're a prophet
we need to stop going *to that dark place*
breathe *duro*
breathe
it's going to be okay
let's center ourselves back to the house of our mind

center

the amount of work i put into something
deserves the same care i need to use when it comes to taking
breaks
sometimes a break is needed, non-negoitable, and important
for my mental health
it's prominent i enjoy the moments i can never get back
enjoy the time with those who supported me from day one

breaks

just because i reflect and write about the past
doesn't mean i let it consume me
let me make it clear to you
i don't want to connect with those same people
it's way of healing certain areas of myself
that i closed off for a long time

the past

.

my poetry isn't everyone
and
that's okay
maybe they'll revisit back when they need it
poetry is constantly changing
and
it's important to fuel our souls with material that connects with
us most
to be okay with this marks the life of an artist

artist

the way you lie to yourself by
refusing to acknowledge the negative signs
isn't only denial
but
is also an act of abuse

the way you lie

i began laughing at all the places that i once cried
the moments where i experienced break-ups, rejections
from jobs or publishers, restrooms that had a mirror that i spoke
negatively about myself - i laughed in all those spots
to reclaim my power
to give myself the ability to walk to those areas without feeling
any animosity towards it
the horseshoe we called it in college
is where i threw my ring he gave me
it was a place i avoided because of the talks we had
it wasn't until one random night
i had an idea like most of us college kids do
i called my friends to come with me
we walked to the horseshoe
i grabbed the ring
and
i felt like a professional baseball player
with how far i threw the ring
my friends cheering me on
we laughed and hugged each other
it was from then on i decided i am going to unlearn those
pessimistic interactions
i once had and reclaim those areas with solace

to laugh made me whole

we're like a table game of dominos
finding the right number to match the end
the strategy and carefulness
the dominos are flipped upside down - a mystery to the eye
we draw seven each
finding the number that is the same as the one placed down
when you don't have matching number
you simply tap the table
signaling to me everything i need to know
this is a game where community and relationships are built and
sustained

el domino de PR

majority of my entire life
i only grew up embracing my mexican heritage
however
when i share with other puerto ricans that i'm also puerto rican
they tell me
that's amazing, what are some of your favorite boricua dishes
yet
it's still hard for me to connect
it wasn't until i was eighteen that i learned of my boricua side
being fully grown now
it inspires me to learn this part of myself
the food, culture, and traditions
when they say *ah, a fellow boricua*
my heart is warm
to be mexicana y boricua
is something i'm excited to share with others and incorporate
into my life
it inspires me to come closer to all my roots
it's never too late and i'm happy i'm taking the steps to do so
little by little

identity

Diosa

there's no *one* way to be latina
we all come in different forms
to balance su familia
y su carrera
isn't easy
the generations of women
we saw around us
were the heroines
now we are passed the crown
to wear proudly
as we venture adulthood
the future relies on our power
to break boundaries
so sit in your power
in your throne amiga

latinahood

it is our birthright to be successful
it is our birthright to be fearless
through it all

our right

amigahood
i love being a big hermana to my amigas
and them being one to me
it's a beautiful circle
that is a force unbreakable
i love being a big hermana to my amigas
when they need a shoulder to lean on
when they need me to be their hypewoman
when they dance, sing, and jump with me
when we share all of the trivial and intimate parts of our lives
when we make each other feel validated
and
feel safe to cry together
i love being a big hermana to my extended family
this is amigahood

amigahood

the echos of my past whisper to me
they want me to react with anger
but those doors i've reopened
i have forgiven those areas of my life
to heal the young girl
it is a gift of release

for her

this body is a healer
she's a giver, lover, and creator

diosa es una mujer

EPILOGUE

Thank you for coming to the end and for reading my collection of poetry.

DIOSA is the sequel of my poetic work as an Author, Artist, and Writer. This collection alongside, *BESOS* means so much to me. This collection of work began development when my first book launched in 2022. It took me three years to write, edit, and even change this book entirely. One of my favorite things when it comes to poetry is that when you decide to not use certain poems or lines in a current project, you can always explore them for future work. Like my last book, I decided to create five separate sections that explore and bring the reader into different chapters into my life. The style and choice to choose to write in lowercase for this book breaks formal traditional rules. It allows the reader to gather a scope closer into this story. It allows the readers to engage, connect, and reflect on each poem in an intimate and personal level. The short poems in this book believe or not were my hardest to edit it due to the length I gave them. Each word was thoughtfully written, so that if I were to remove the other words, each word itself in the line can stand on its own to carry power.

The meaning of *DIOSA* for me means a variety of things - from writing this I learned that I can be both soft and powerful. I know where to let both of those traits shine independently and collectively. It other meanings, it also represents the beauty and home that is our body and how we should honor it. I hope these poems were able to give you healing, comfort, and ultimately a home within you. I know they did for me.

¡Gracias por tu apoyo!

Con Amor,
Celeste Alyssa Gomez

To follow for more of my work you can do so here:
Instagram: **@celestealyssagomez**
Website: **www.lapoetapublications.com**

ABOUT THE AUTHOR

LA-based Latina Poet and Author, Celeste Alyssa Gomez, is a ground-breaking performer who rose from the world of self-publishing. She completed her first tour in 2025 called *Los Recuerdos* - a tour highlighting the poetry within Celeste's first book, *BESOS. BESOS* is available in both English and Spanish and has been featured in various articles/podcasts like *HipLatina, Harness Magazine, Latina Leadership,* and more. It's in various bookstores within the U.S. and internationally, including big retailers like Barnes & Noble. Her other work includes the *CHISMOSA* Zine, where she's a co-editor as well as being a co-founder for the *Hermosa y Libros Book Festival.*

Celeste signed with Alegría Publishing in July 2025 to produce *DIOSA.* Alegría Publishing is one of the most notable publishers that focuses on publishing Latine/x stories and supporting new emerging voices. Alegría is a community that connects, inspires, and highlights the beauty, the lineage, the thousands of years of positive contributions to this planet by artists & leaders of color.

You can follow them on Instagram @alegriapublishing
To follow for more of Celeste's work you can do so here:
Instagram: **@celestealyssagomez**
Website: **www.lapoetapublications.com**